MW00719188

Because you are but a young man, beware of temptations and snares; and above all, be careful to keep yourself in the use of means; resort to good company; and howbeit you be nicknamed a Puritan, and mocked, yet care not for that, but rejoice and be glad, that they who are scorned and scoffed by this godless and vain world, and nicknamed Puritans, would admit you to their society; for I must tell you, when I am at this point as you see me, I get no comfort to my soul by any second means under heaven but from those who are nicknamed Puritans. They are the men that can give a word of comfort to a wearied soul in due season, and that I have found by experience . . .

THE LAST AND HEAVENLY SPEECHES, AND
GLORIOUS DEPARTURE, OF JOHN, VISCOUNT KENMURE

THE
TENDER HEART

Richard Sibbes

THE BANNER OF TRUTH TRUST

THE BANNER OF TRUTH TRUST

Head Office
3 Murrayfield Road
Edinburgh, EH12 6EL
UK

North America Office
PO Box 621
Carlisle, PA 17013
USA

banneroftruth.org

*

ISBN 978 1 84871 105 1

*

Typeset in 10.5/13.5 pt Adobe Caslon Pro
at The Banner of Truth Trust, Edinburgh

Printed in the USA by
Versa Press, Inc.,
East Peoria, IL

*

Taken from *Josiah's Reformation* in
The Works of Richard Sibbes
(Edinburgh: Banner of Truth, repr. 1983)
vol. 6, pp. 29-43

The original text has been lightly edited
so as to modernize archaic pronouns and verb forms.

FOREWORD

Richard Sibbes (1577-1635)—the 'heavenly Doctor' as he came to be called—was a man who clearly enjoyed knowing God. And even centuries later, his relish is infectious. He spoke of the living God as a life-giving, warming sun who 'delights to spread his beams and his influence in inferior things, to make all things fruitful. Such a goodness is in God as is in a fountain, or in the breast that loves to ease itself of milk.'

And knowing God to be such an over-flowing fountain of goodness and love made him a most attractive model of God-likeness. For, he said, 'those that are led with the Spirit of God, that are like him; they have a communicative, diffusive goodness that loves to spread itself.' In other words, knowing God's love, he became loving; and his understanding of who God is transformed him into a man, a preacher, and a writer of magnetic geniality. He was never married, but looking at his life, it is clear that he had a quite extraordinary ability for cultivating warm and lasting friendships. Charles Spurgeon once told his students that he loved the sort of minister whose face invites you to be his friend, the sort of face on which you read the sign 'Welcome' and not 'Beware of the dog'. He could have been describing Sibbes.

Sibbes was born to a wheelwright in a rather obscure little village in Suffolk. Few could have expected how influential young Sibbes would turn out to be. Before long, though, it was clear that he was remarkably capable: sailing through his studies at Cambridge, he became a tutor at St John's College aged only twenty-four. Bright as he was, though, it was his ability as a preacher that soon began to mark him out. Before long, he was appointed to be a 'lecturer' at Holy Trinity Church in Cambridge (where a gallery had to be built to accommodate the extra numbers he attracted), and a few years later he was appointed to be a preacher at Gray's Inn, one of the London Inns of Court where many soon-to-be-influential men of Puritan persuasion came to hear him.

Knowing, as he once said, that there is more grace in Christ than there is sin in us, he always sought in his preaching to win the hearts of his listeners to Christ. This, he believed, was the special duty of ministers: 'they woo for Christ, and open the riches, beauty, honour, and all that is lovely in him.' The result was preaching so winsome that struggling believers began to call him the 'honey-mouthed', the 'sweet dropper', and, apparently, hardened sinners deliberately avoided his sermons for fear he would convert them. One listener, Humphrey Mills, recorded his experience of Sibbes's ministry, and it seems to have been typical:

I was for three years together wounded for sins, and under a sense of my corruptions, which were many; and I followed sermons, pursuing the means, and was constant in duties and doing; looking for Heaven that way. And then I was so precise for outward formalities, that I censured all to be reprobates, that wore their hair anything long, and not short above their ears; or that wore great ruffs, and gorgets, or fashions, and follies. But yet I was distracted in my mind, wounded in conscience, and wept often and bitterly, and prayed earnestly, but yet had no comfort, till I heard that sweet saint . . . Doctor Sibbs, by whose means and ministry I was brought to peace and joy in my spirit. His sweet soul-melting Gospel-sermons won my heart and refreshed me much, for by him I saw and had much of God and was confident in Christ, and could overlook the world . . . my heart held firm and resolved and my desires all heaven-ward.

In 1626, Sibbes was appointed Master of Katharine Hall, Cambridge, and for the last decade of his life he would use his considerable influence to promote his

Christ-centred theology. He sought to place trusted Puritan preachers in church teaching posts around the country; he personally nurtured a number of young ministers, men such as Thomas Goodwin, John Cotton, Jeremiah Burroughs, John Preston, and Philip Nye; and through his printed sermons he affected countless more.

Richard Sibbes was not the first Puritan I read (I started with John Owen), but to my mind Sibbes is actually the best introduction to the Puritans. And ever since the day when, as a student, I read his *The Bruised Reed,* Sibbes has been my favourite. 'Sibbes never wastes the student's time,' wrote Spurgeon, 'he scatters pearls and diamonds with both hands.' Reading him is like sitting in the sunshine: he gets into your heart and warms it to Christ.

This little book was originally the first sermon in a four-part series entitled *Josiah's Reformation* (available as a whole in the Banner of Truth 'Puritan Paperback' series). In it, Sibbes expounds 2 Chronicles 34:26-27, where the Lord is said to have heard Josiah because his heart was tender.

'The Tender Heart' is foundational, not only for the rest of the series, but for all of Sibbes's theology. In his ministry, Sibbes always sought to get under the superficial layer of his listeners' behaviour and deal with their hearts, their affections and their desires. For Sibbes, this was no secondary matter, the devotional clothes his theology wore. Rather, in looking to deal with the heart, he believed he was preserving one of the most profound insights of the Reformation of which he was a part.

Again and again in his sermons, Sibbes speaks of both Catholic priests and Protestant pastors who—whatever their professed theology—act as though the root of our problem before God lies in our behaviour: we have done wrong things and we need to start doing right things. Sibbes plumbs much deeper. He knew that the outward acts of sin are merely the manifestations of the inner desires of the heart. Merely to alter a person's behaviour without dealing with those desires would cultivate hypocrisy, the self-righteous cloak for a cold and vicious heart. And, Sibbes would note, ministries that worked like that were invariably cruel, based on brow-beating. No, hearts must be turned, and evil desires eclipsed by stronger ones for Christ.

In 'The Tender Heart', then, Sibbes sets about the deepest possible work—of heart-surgery. He explains that those who are tender-hearted—who are soft to the Lord—do not simply desire 'salvation'; they desire the Lord of salvation himself. Only then, when a person is brought to love the Lord with heart-felt sincerity, will they truly begin to hate their sin instead of merely dreading the thought of God's punishment of it. In all this, Sibbes displays just how beautiful, pure, and desirable a soft heart is, and by his honesty and kindness, he heaps burning coals on hypocrisy, making you mourn your own hard-heartedness as you feel what a wretched thing it is.

Then, having whetted your appetite for such a heart, he shows you how hearts can be made tender:

> Tenderness of heart is wrought by an apprehension of tenderness and love in

Christ. A soft heart is made soft by the blood of Christ. (p. 21 below)

As when things are cold we bring them to the fire to heat and melt, so we bring our cold hearts to the fire of the love of Christ. (p. 57 below)

If you will have this tender and melting heart, then use the means of grace; be always under the sunshine of the gospel. (p. 57 below)

Not only is Sibbes beautifully capturing the warmth and joy of hearty holiness; he is also making a most significant point. That is, we are sanctified just as we were first saved—through believing in Christ. By revealing Christ to me, the Spirit turns my heart from its natural hatred of God towards a sincere love for him. Only thereby can my heart be made tender. Sibbes once said to Thomas Goodwin, 'Young man, if ever you would do good, you must preach the gospel and the free grace of God in Christ Jesus.' He meant it with every fibre of his being, for he saw that the free grace of God in Christ Jesus is the means by which the hearts of sinners are first turned to God, and the means by which the hearts of believers continue to be turned from the love of sin to love of God.

I don't think I can exaggerate the importance of 'The Tender Heart' and its message for today. Our busyness and activism so easily degenerate into a hypocrisy in which we keep up all the appearance of holiness without the heart of it. Ministers can bludgeon their people into such hollow Christianity, and even use Christ as a package to pass on to others, instead of enjoying him first and foremost as their own Saviour. But true reformation—whether reformation in Josiah's day, Sibbes's, or ours—must begin in the heart, with love for Christ. And that can only come when the free grace of God in Christ Jesus is preached.

Richard Sibbes was a bright lantern of the Reformation, and he knew the issues dealt with in this book to be essential to the work of reform. Oh, may it reform you as you read it, and foster reformation in our day!

MICHAEL REEVES

THE TENDER HEART

*And as for the king of Judah, who sent you
to inquire of the LORD, so shall you say unto
him, Thus says the LORD God of Israel concerning the words which you have heard,
Because your heart was tender, etc.*

2 Chron. 34:26–27.

These words are a part of the message
which the prophetess Huldah sent
to good King Josiah; for as the message
was concerning him and his people, so his

answer from her is exact, both for himself and them. That part which concerned his people is set down in the three foregoing verses; that which belongs unto himself is contained in the words now read unto you, 'But to the king of Judah, *etc.*' The preface to her message we see strengthened with authority from God, 'Thus says the LORD God of Israel'; which words carry in them the greater force and power from the majesty of the author. For if words spoken from a king carry authority, how much more then the word of the Lord of hosts, the King of kings? Here is her wisdom, therefore, that she lays aside her own authority, and speaks in the name of the Lord.

We see that waters of the same colour have not the same nature and effect, for hot waters are of the same colour with plain ordinary waters, yet more effectual; so the words of a man coming from a man may seem at first to be the same with others, yet notwithstanding, the words of God coming from the Spirit of God carry a more wonderful excellency in them even to the hearts of kings. They bind kings, though they labour to shake them off. They are arrows to pierce their hearts; if not to save them, yet to damn them. Therefore she speaks to the king, 'Thus says the LORD God of Israel concerning the words which you have heard, *etc.*'

Here we read of Josiah, that he was a man of an upright heart, and one who did that which was right in the sight of the Lord; and answerably we find the Lord to deal with him. For he, desirous to know the issue of a fearful judgment threatened against him and his people, sends to Huldah, the prophetess of the Lord, to be certified therein; whereupon he receives the full and perfect answer of the Lord's determination, both touching himself and his people, that they being forewarned might be forearmed; and by their timely conversion to the Lord, might procure the aversion[1] of so heavy wrath. He in uprightness sends to inquire, and the Lord returns him a full and upright answer. Whence we may learn,

Doctrine. 1. *That God graciously fits prophets for persons, and his word to a people that are upright in their hearts.* Where there is a true desire to know the will of God, there God will give men sincere prophets that shall answer them exactly; not according to

---

[1] That is, 'turning away'.

their own lusts, but for their good. Josiah was an holy man, who, out of a gracious disposition, desirous to be informed from God what should become of him and his people, sends to the prophetess Huldah. It was God's mercy that he should have a Huldah, a Jeremiah, to send to; and it was God's mercy that they should deal faithfully with him. This is God's mercy to those that are true-hearted. He will give them teachers suitable to their desires; but those that are false-hearted shall have suitable teachers, who shall instruct them according to their lusts. If they be like Ahab, they shall have four hundred false prophets to teach falsehood, to please their lusts (*1 Kings* 22:6); but if they be Davids, they shall have Nathans. If they be Josiahs, they shall have Huldahs and Jeremiahs. Indeed,

Herod may have a John the Baptist (*Mark* 6:27); but what will he do with him in the end when he comes to cross him in his sin? Then off goes his head!

Application. This should teach us *to labour for sincerity, to have our hearts upright towards God;* and then he will send us men of a direct and right spirit, that shall teach us according to his own heart. But if we be false-hearted, God will give us teachers that shall teach us, not according to his will, but to please our own. We shall light upon belly-gods and Epicureans, and shall fall into the hands of priests and Jesuits. Where such are, there are the judgments of God upon the people, because they do not desire to know the will of God in truth. We see (*Ezek.* 14:3, 4) the people desired to have a stumblingblock for their iniquity. They were wicked and would have idols. There-fore they desired stumblingblocks. They would have false prophets, that so they might go to hell with some authority. Well, says God, they shall have stumblingblocks: for thus says the Lord God of Israel, 'To every man that sets up his idols in his heart, and puts the stumblingblock of his iniquity before his face, and comes to the prophet to inquire; I the Lord will answer him that comes, according to the multitude of his idols; according to his own false heart, and not according to good.' What brought the greatest judgment upon the world, next to hell itself, I mean antichrist—the terriblest judgment of all, that has drawn so many souls to hell—but the wickedness of the place and people, and his own ambition? The sins of the people gave life to him. They could not endure the word of God or plain dealing; they thought it a simple thing. They must have more sacrifices, more ceremonies, and a more glorious government. They would not be content with Christ's government which he left them, but were weary of this. Therefore, he being gone to heaven, they must have a pope to go before them and lead them to hell. Therefore let men never excuse those sins, for certainly God saw a great deal of evil in them and therefore gave them up to the judgment of antichrist. But let us magnify God's mercies that have not so given us up. Thus we see how graciously God deals with a true-hearted king: he sends him a true answer of his message.

Verse 27, 'Because your heart was tender, *etc.*'

Now here comes a comfortable message to good Josiah, that he should be taken away and not see the miseries that should befall his people; the cause whereof is here set down, 'Because your heart was tender and you humbled yourself before God'; which cause is double.

1. *Inward.* 2. *Outward.*

1. The inward is the tenderness of his heart and humbling of himself.

2. And then, the outward expression of it is set down in a double act: (1.) Rending of clothes. (2.) Weeping.

'Because you have torn your clothes, and wept before me.' After which comes the promise, 'I have also heard you,' says the Lord; 'behold, I will gather you to your fathers, and you shall be put in your grave in peace, and your eyes shall not see all the evil which I will bring upon this place, and upon the inhabitants of the same.'

I will first remove one doubt, before I come to the tenderness of Josiah's heart.

Question. What! may some say, Is there anything in man that can cause God to do him good?

Answer. No. One thing is the cause of another, but all come from the first cause. So tenderness of heart may be some cause of removal of judgment; but God is the cause of both, for they all come from the first cause: which is God. So that these words do rather contain an order than a cause. For God has set down this order in things, that where there is a broken heart there shall be a freedom from judgment; not that tenderness of heart deserves anything at God's hand, as the papists gather, but because God has decreed it so, that where tenderness of heart is, there mercy shall follow; as here there was a tender heart in Josiah, therefore mercy did follow. God's promises are made conditionally; not that the condition on our part deserves anything at God's hand, but when God has given the condition, he gives the thing promised. So that this is an order which God has set down, that where there is grace, mercy shall follow. For where God intends to do any good, he first works in them a gracious disposition: after which he looks upon his own work as upon a lovely object, and so gives them other blessings. God crowns grace with grace.

By 'heart' is not meant the inward material and fleshy part of the body; but that spiritual part, the soul and affections thereof. In that it is said to be 'tender' or melting, it is a borrowed and metaphorical phrase. Now in a 'tender heart' these three properties concur:

1. It is sensible. 2. It is pliable. 3. It is yielding.

1. First, A tender heart is always a *sensible*[2] heart. It has life and therefore sense. There is no living creature but has life, and sense to preserve that life. So a tender heart is sensible of any grievance; for tenderness presupposes life, because nothing that has not life is tender. Some senses are not altogether necessary for the being of a living creature, as hearing and seeing; but sensibleness is needful to the being of every living creature. It is a sign of life in a Christian when he is sensible of inconveniences. Therefore God has planted such affections

[2] That is, 'able to sense, feel; sensitive'.

in man, as may preserve the life of man, as fear and love. Fear is that which makes a man avoid many dangers. Therefore God has given us fear to cause us to make our peace with him in time, that we may be freed from inconveniences; yea, from that greatest of inconveniences, hell fire.

2, 3. Again, A tender heart is *pliable and yielding*. Now that is said to be yielding and pliable, which yields to the touch of anything that is put to it, and does not stand out, as a stone that rebounds back when it is thrown against a wall. So that is said to be tender which has life, and sense, and is pliable, as wax is yielding and pliable to the disposition of him that works it, and is apt to receive any impression that is applied to it. In a tender heart there is no resistance, but it yields presently to every truth, and has a pliableness and a fitness to receive any impression, and to execute any performance; a fit temper indeed for a heart wrought on by the Spirit. God must first make us fit, and then use us to work. As a wheel must first be made round, and then turned round, so the head must be first altered, and then used in a renewed way. A tender heart, so soon as the word is spoken, yields to it. It quakes at threatenings, obeys precepts, melts at promises, and the promises sweeten the heart. In all duties concerning God, and all offices of love to man, a tender heart is thus qualified. But hardness of heart is quite opposite. For, as things dead and insensible, it will not yield to the touch, but returns back whatsoever is cast upon it. Such a heart may be broken in pieces, but it will not receive any impression; as a stone may be broken, but will not be pliable, but rebound back again. A hard heart is indeed like wax to the devil, but like a stone to God or goodness. It is not yielding, but resists and repels all that is good; and therefore compared in the Scripture to the adamant stone. Sometimes it is called a frozen heart, because it is unpliable to anything. You may break it in pieces, but it is unframeable for any service, for any impression; it will not be wrought upon. But on the contrary, a melting and tender heart is sensible, yielding, and fit for any service both to God and man. Thus we see plainly what a tender heart is. The point from hence is,

Doctrine 2. *That it is a supernatural disposition of a true child of God to have a tender, soft, and melting heart.* I say that a disposition of a true child of God, and the frame of soul of such an one, to be tender, apprehensive, and serviceable, is a supernatural disposition; and of necessity it must be so, because naturally the heart is of another temper—a stony heart. All by nature have stony hearts in respect of spiritual goodness. There may be a tenderness in regard of natural things; but in regard of grace, the heart is stony, and beats back all that is put to it. Say what you will to a hard heart, it will never yield. A hammer will do no good to a stone. It may break it in pieces, but not draw it to any form. So to a stony heart, all the threatenings in the world will do no good. You may break it in pieces, but never work upon it. It must be the almighty power of God. There is nothing in the world so hard as the heart of man. The very creatures will yield obedience to God; as flies, and lice, to destroy Pharaoh; but Pharaoh himself was so hard-hearted, that after ten plagues he was ten times the more hardened (*Exod.* 10:28). Therefore, if a man have not a melting heart, he is diverted from his proper object; because God has placed affections in us, to be raised presently upon suitable objects. When any object is offered in the word of God, if our hearts were not corrupted, we would have correspondent affections. At judgments we would tremble, at the word of threatenings quake, at promises we would with faith believe, and at mercies be comforted; at directions we would be pliable and yielding. But by nature our hearts are hard. God, may threaten, and promise, and direct, and yet we be insensible all the while. Well, all Josiahs, and all that are gracious, of necessity must have soft hearts. Therefore I will show you, 1. *How a tender heart is wrought.* 2. *How it may be preserved and maintained.* 3. *How it may be discerned from the contrary.*

1. First, A tender heart is made tender *by him that made it.* For no creature in the world can soften and turn the heart, only God must alter and change it; for we are all by nature earthly, dead, and hard. Hence is it that God makes that gracious promise (*Ezek.* 11:19), 'I will give them one heart, and put a new spirit within them; and I will take away the stony hearts out of their bodies, and give them a heart of flesh', that is, a living, sensible heart.

Question. But does God immediately make the heart tender, and change it, without any help by means?

Solution 1. I answer, Means do not make the heart tender, but God through the use of means softens it by his word. God's word is a hammer to break, and as fire to melt the hardened heart (*Jer.* 23:29). And thus it works, first, when God shows to the heart our cursed estate, and opens to the same the true dangers of the soul, which it is in by nature and custom of sin, and sets before it the terrors of the last day and present danger of judgment. When the Spirit of God, by the word, convinces the soul to be in a damned estate, dead, born under wrath, and an heir of damnation; that by nature God frowns, and hell is ready to swallow us up; when the soul is thus convinced, then the heart begins to be astonished, and cries out, 'Men and brethren, what shall I do?' (*Acts* 2:37). When the word is thus preached with particular application, it does good. For a man may hear the word of God generally, and yet have no broken heart. But when a Peter comes and says, 'You have crucified the Lord of life'; and when a Nathan comes to David, and says, 'You are the man', then comes the heart to be broken and confounded.

But it is not enough to have the heart broken; for a pot may be broken in pieces, and yet be good for nothing; so may a heart be, through terrors, and sense of judgment, and yet not be like wax, pliable. Therefore it must be melted; for which cause, when God by his judgments has cast down the heart, then comes the Spirit of God, revealing the comfort of the word; then the gracious mercy of God in Christ is manifested, that 'there is mercy with God, that he may be feared' (*Psa.* 130:4). This being laid open to the quick, to a dejected soul, hence it comes to be melted and tender; for the apprehension of judgment is only a preparing work, which breaks the heart, and prepares it for tenderness.

Solution 2. Again, tenderness of heart is wrought by an apprehension of tenderness and love in Christ. A soft heart is made soft by the blood of Christ. Many say, that an adamant cannot be melted with fire, but by blood. I cannot tell whether this be true or not; but I am sure nothing will melt the hard heart of man but the blood of Christ, the passion of our blessed Saviour. When a man considers of the love that God has showed him in sending of his Son, and doing such great things as he has done, in giving of Christ to satisfy his justice, in setting us free from hell, Satan and death: the consideration of this, with the persuasion that we have interest in the same, melts the heart, and makes it become tender. And this must needs be so, because that with the preaching of the gospel unto broken-hearted sinners cast down, there always goes the Spirit of God, which works an application of the gospel.

Christ is the first gift to the church. When God has given Christ, then comes the Spirit, and works in the heart a gracious acceptance of mercy offered. The Spirit works an assurance of the love and mercy of God. Now love and mercy felt, work upon the tender heart a reflective love to God again. What! Has the great God of heaven and earth sent Christ into the world for me? humbled himself to the death of the cross for me? and has he let angels alone, and left many thousands in the world, to choose me? and has he sent his ministers to reveal unto me this assurance of the love and mercy of God? This consideration cannot but work love to God again; for love is a kind of fire which melts the heart. So that when our souls are persuaded that God loves us from everlasting, then we reflect our love to him again; and then our heart says to God, 'Speak, Lord; what will you have me to do?' The soul is pliable for doing, for suffering, for anything God will have it. Then, 'Speak, Lord, for your servant hears' (*1 Sam.* 3:9).

And when the heart is thus wrought upon, and made tender by the Spirit, then afterward in the proceeding of our lives, many things will work tenderness: as the works of God, his judgments, the word and sacraments, when they are made effectual by the Spirit of God, work tenderness. The promises of God also make the heart tender, as Romans 12:1, 'I beseech you, brethren, by the mercies of God, offer up your souls and bodies a living sacrifice, holy and acceptable unto God.' There is no such like argument to persuade men to tenderness of heart, as to propound the love and mercy of God. And so the fear of any judgment will work tenderness. This made Josiah's heart to melt, but yet this did not work first upon him; for he having a tender heart before, and being sure of God's love, when he heard the judgment that should come upon his people, out of love to God and to his people, his heart melted, not so much for fear of judgment, but to think that God should be provoked by the sins of his people.

And thus we have seen how tenderness of heart is wrought. Now I come to show,

2. *Second, The means how we may preserve this tenderness of heart,* because it is a disposition of God's children. How then shall we preserve ourselves in such a perpetual temper? The way to preserve a tender heart is,

1. First, *To be under the means whereby God's Spirit will work;* for it is he by his Spirit that works upon the heart, and preserves tenderness in us; and he will work only by his own means. All the devices in the world will not work upon the heart. Therefore let us be under the means that may preserve tenderness, and hear what God's word says of our estate by nature, of the wrath and justice of God, and of the judgment that will shortly come upon all the world. This made

Paul to cry, though he knew that he was the child of God, and free from the law. 'Therefore', says he, 'knowing the terror of the Lord, we admonish you' (*2 Cor.* 5:11).

2. And then, *go into the house of mourning, and present before yourselves the miserable and forlorn estate of the church of God abroad.* It was this that broke Nehemiah's heart. When he heard that the Jews were in great affliction and reproach, that the wall of the city was broken down, and the gates thereof burnt with fire, he sat down and wept, and mourned certain days, fasted and prayed before the God of heaven (*Neh.* 1:4). This made this good man Nehemiah to mourn, so that all the princes of the court could not comfort him. This also made Moses's heart to melt, when he looked on his brethren's affliction in Egypt. So we might keep

our hearts tender if we did but set before our eyes the pitiful estate of God's church abroad, and that we may come to be in such an estate ourselves before long.

3. And if you will preserve tenderness of heart, *labour for a legal and evangelical faith.* We must believe that all the threatenings of God's vengeance against the wicked shall come to pass. Faith makes these things present before our eyes; for it is the nature of faith to set things absent as present before us. What makes the malefactor to tremble and be cast down, but when he sees that he is ready for to die, is going to the place of execution, and sees death look him in the face? So faith setting the day of judgment before our eyes, will make us to tremble. Therefore Paul so often adjures Timothy by the coming of the Lord Jesus

to judgment (*2 Tim.* 4:1); and Enoch set the Day of Judgment before him, at the beginning of the world, as we may see in Jude 14. He had a faith, that set things to come as present, and made him to walk with God. So if we had an evangelical faith to believe the goodness of God, pardon from him, and everlasting life, this would preserve tenderness of heart.

4. Again, *Good company will preserve tenderness of heart, sorting ourselves with those that are tender-hearted.* For the soul will reason thus: Does such an one make conscience of swearing, profaning the Sabbath? and does he mourn for the miseries of the church? Then what a hard piece of dead flesh am I, that have nothing in me!

5. Again, If you would preserve tenderness of heart, by all means *take heed of the*

least sin against conscience, for the least sin in this kind makes way for hardness of heart. Sins that are committed against conscience do darken the understanding, deaden the affection, and take away life; so that one has not the least strength to withstand the least temptation. And so it comes to pass by God's judgment; for when men will live in sins against conscience, he takes away his Spirit, and gives up the heart from one degree of hardness to another. For the heart at first being tender, will endure nothing, but the least sin will trouble it. As water, when it begins to freeze, will not endure anything, no not so much as the weight of a pin upon it, but after a while will bear the weight of a cart; even so at the beginning, the heart being tender, trembles at the least sin, and will not bear with any one;

but when it once gives way to sins against conscience, it becomes so frozen that it can endure any sin, and so becomes more and more hard. Men are so obdurate, having once made a breach in their own hearts by sins against conscience, that they can endure to commit any sin; and therefore God gives them up from one degree of hardness to another. What will not men do whom God has given up to hardness of heart?

6. Again, If you will preserve tenderness of heart, *take heed of spiritual drunkenness;* that is, that you be not drunk with an immoderate use of created things; of setting your love too much upon outward things. For what says the prophet? 'Wine and women take away the heart' (*Hos.* 4:11); that is, the immoderate use of

any earthly thing takes away spiritual sense; for the more sensible the soul is of outward things, the less it is of spiritual. For as the outward takes away the inward heat, so the love of one thing abates the love of another. The setting of too much love upon earthly things, takes away the sense of better things, and hardens the heart. When the heart is filled with the pleasures and profits of this life, it is not sensible of any judgment that hangs over the head; as in the old world, they ate and drank, they married and gave in marriage, they bought and sold, while the flood came upon them and swept all away (*Matt.* 24:37). When a man sets his love upon created things, the very strength of his soul is lost. Therefore in the Scripture, God joins prayer and fasting together (*Matt.* 17:21); that when he would have our hearts raised up to heaven, we should have all use of earthly things taken away. Therefore when we are to go about spiritual duties, we must cut ourselves short in the use of created things. Talk of religion to a carnal man, whose senses are lost with love of earthly things, he has no ear for that; his sense is quite lost, he has no relish or savour of anything that is good. Talk to a covetous man, that has his soul set upon the things of this life, he has no relish of anything else; his heart is already so hardened to get honour and wealth, though it be to the ruin of others, that he cares not how hard it become. Therefore we are bidden to take heed that our hearts be not overcome with drunkenness and the cares of this life, for these will make a man to be insensible of spiritual things (*Luke* 21:34).

7. Again, If you will preserve tenderness of heart, *take heed of hypocrisy;* for it causes swelling, and pride makes the heart to despise others that be not like unto us. They bless themselves that they live thus and thus, they think themselves better than any other; and if they hear the minister reprove them for sin, they will shift it off, and say, Oh, this belongs not to me, but to such a carnal man, and to such a wicked person; as the Scribes and Pharisees, who were vile hypocrites, yet they were the cause of all mischief, and more hard-hearted than Pilate, an heathen man; for he would have delivered Christ, but they would not (*Luke* 23:14–23). So, take a Romish hypocrite, that can proudly compliment it at every word with enticing speech, yet you shall find him more hard-hearted than Turk or Jew; for

full of cruelty and blood is the 'whore of Babylon'. Therefore, if you will have tenderness of heart, take heed of hypocrisy.

8. Again, Above all things, *take heed of great sins,* which will harden the heart; for little sins do many times not deaden the heart, but stir up the conscience; but great sins do stun and dull a man; as a prick of a pin will make a man to start, but a heavy blow makes a man for to be dead for the present. Therefore take heed of great sins. Thus it was with David. He sinned in numbering of the people, and for this his heart smote him; but when he came to the great and devouring sin of Uriah and Bathsheba, this was a great blow that struck him and laid him for dead, till Nathan came and revived him (*2 Sam.* 12:1). For when men fall into great sins, their hearts are so hardened,

that they go on from sin to sin. Let us therefore be watchful over our own hearts, to preserve tenderness. The eye being a tender part, and soonest hurt, how watchful is man by nature over that, that it take no hurt. So the heart, being a tender thing, let us preserve it by all watchfulness to keep blows from off it. It is a terrible thing to keep a wound of some great sin upon the conscience, for it makes a way for a new breach; because when the conscience once begins to be hardened with some great sin, then there is no stop, but we run on to commit sin with all greediness.

9. Lastly, If you will preserve tenderness of heart, *consider the miserable estate of hardness of heart.* Such an one that has an hard heart is next to hell itself, to the estate of a damned spirit, a most terrible estate. A

hard heart is neither melted with promises nor broken with threatenings. He has no feelings of pity to men or love to God. He forgets all judgment for things past, and looks for none to come. When the soul is in this case, it is fit for nothing but for sin and the devil, whereas a tender-hearted man is fit for all good. Let God threaten: he trembles and quakes; let God promise: his heart melts and rejoices, and makes him even to break forth into thanksgiving; let God command: he will perform all; he is fit for any good thing to God and man. But when a man's heart is hardened by hypocrisy, covetousness, or custom in sin, he has no pity, no compassion: let God command, threaten, or promise, yet the heart is never in the least moved. This is a terrible estate of soul.

Now, to speak a little to *young men* that are like to this holy man Josiah. Surely his tenderness had some advantage from his years. Let those that are young by all means labour to keep tenderness of heart; for if young persons be good, there is a sweet communion between God and them, before the heart be pestered with the cares of the world. God delights much in the prayers of young men, because they come not from so polluted a soul, hardened with the practices of this world. Let such, therefore, as are young, take advantage of it, to repent in time of their sins, and let them not put it off unto their old days. While we are young, let us not neglect natural tenderness; although we cannot bring ourselves under the compass of God's kingdom by it, yet shall we get our hearts the sooner to be tender. In our youth, therefore, let us not neglect this good opportunity, as good Josiah did not when he was but young. Therefore let us repent of every sin speedily, and acquaint ourselves with those that are good; as it is said, 'Let us provoke one another daily, while it is called today, lest any of you be hardened through the deceitfulness of sin' (*Heb.* 3:13). Let us use all means to keep our hearts tender. Oh, it is a blessed estate! We are fit to live when our hearts are tender; fit to die, fit to receive anything from God, fit for duties of honesty to men, for any service to God. But when we have lost sense and feeling, it must be the almighty power of God that must recover us again, and not one amongst an hundred comes to good. Therefore labour to preserve a tender, soft, and melting heart.

Now, before I proceed, give me leave to answer some cases of conscience, as:

Question 1. First, Whether the children of God may be subject to this hardness of heart, opposed to this tenderness?

Question 2. Secondly, Whether a Christian may be more sensible of outward things than of spiritual, as the love of God, or his own sin, and the like?

Solution 1. To the first I answer, *that the child of God may be hard-hearted.* He may have some degrees of hardness of heart in him. For a Christian is a compounded creature; he has not only body and soul, but flesh and spirit. He is but in part renewed; and therefore, having in him both flesh and spirit, he is subject to hardness of heart; and it is clear that it may be so. Examples show that God's children are not always alike sensible of the wrath of God and of his mercy. They do not yield so to his commands as they should. But what is the reason that God suffers his children to fall into this hardness of heart? There is something in us that makes him give us up unto it, for we are no longer soft than he works upon us.

Question. But what moves him to leave us in this disposition?

Solution. I answer, he does it for correction of former negligences, for sins of omission; especially when they neglect some means of grace whereby their hearts might be kept tender: it is for want of stirring up of God's grace in them; for want of an high esteem of grace bestowed upon them; want of care of their company, for not associating themselves with such as are

tender-hearted; and from hence it comes
that God suffers his children to fall into
hardness of heart.

Question. But now, from hence arises
another question: How may a man know
his heart from the heart of a reprobate, seeing that God's children may have hardness
of heart?

Answer. I answer, that the heart of
a man that is a very reprobate is totally,
wholly, and finally hardened, and it is
joined with security and insensibleness;
it is joined with obstinacy, and with con-
tempt of the means of grace. But the child
of God has not total and final hardness of
heart, but has a sensibleness of it, he feels
and sees it. Total hardness feels nothing,
but a Christian that has hardness of heart,
feels that he has it; as a man that has the

stone in his bladder, feels and knows that he has a stone. A hard-hearted man feels nothing, but he that has but only hardness of heart does feel: for there is difference between hardness of heart and a hard heart; for the child of God may have *hardness of heart*, but not a *hard heart*. Now, I say a child of God that has hardness of heart is sensible of his hardness, and performs the actions of a sensible soul: he uses some good means for the softening of it, for the sense thereof is grievous to him above all other crosses; and while he is under it, he thinks that all is not with him as it should be: therefore he complains of it above all other afflictions, which makes him cry to God, as we may see in Isaiah 63:17: 'Why have you hardened our hearts from your fear?'

Objection. But some may demand how God hardens.

Solution. I answer, the cause is first from our own selves; but he hardens four ways:

1. First, *Privatively,* by withholding and withdrawing his melting and softening power. For as the sun causes darkness by withdrawing his light and warming power, so God withdrawing that melting power whereby we should be softened, it cannot be but that we must needs be hardened.

2. Secondly, *Negatively,* by denying of grace; by taking away from us his graces, which are not natural in us. Thus God does to those whom he absolutely hardens; he takes away that which they have, and so they become worse than they of themselves were by nature. When men walk unworthy

of the gospel, God takes away very rational life from them, and gives them up to hardness of heart, that they run on in such courses, as that they are their own enemies, and bring upon themselves ruin.

3. *Thirdly,* And as God hardens by privation and negation, so, in the third place, he hardens by *tradition:*[3] by giving us up to the devil, to be vexed by his troubles, to harden us. It is a fearful judgment. When we take a course to grieve the Spirit of God, the Spirit will take a course to grieve us: he will give us up to Satan, to blind and to harden us. So that though God does not work, as the author, effectually in this hardening, yet as a just judge he does, by giving us up to Satan and the natural lusts of our

---

[3] That is, 'handing over' or 'giving up'. See also *1 Tim.* 1:20 for the *word*.

own hearts, which are worse than all the devils in hell.

4. Fourthly and lastly, he hardens *objectively,* by propounding good objects, which, meeting with a wicked heart, make it more hard, as it is said, 'Harden these people's hearts' (*Isa.* 6:10). How? By preaching of the word. A good object, if it lights upon a bad soul, hardens the heart; for they that are not bettered by religion, under the means of grace, are so much the worse by their use. So we see God cannot be impeached with the hardening of our hearts, because all the cause is from ourselves; for whether he hardens by privation, negation, tradition, or by propounding good objects, it is all from ourselves; and likewise we have seen that God's children may have hardness of heart in some measure, but yet it differs from

a reprobate, because they see and feel it, grieve for it, and complain of it to God.

Question. The second question is, *But whether may a child of God be more sensible of outward joys or crosses, than of spiritual things?* for this makes many think they have not tender hearts, because they are more sensible of outward things than of spiritual.

Answer. I answer, It is not always alike with them; for God's children are still complaining of something: of their carelessness in good duties, of their want of strength against corruption. They go mourning when they have made God to bring them down upon their knees for their hardness of heart; but there is an intercourse, in the children of God, between the flesh and the spirit. They are partly flesh and partly spirit.

Therefore many times, for a while, when the flesh prevails, there may be a sudden joy and a sudden sorrow, which may be greater than spiritual joy or spiritual sorrow; but yet it is not continual. But spiritual sorrow, grief for sin, though it be not so vehement as, for the sudden, outward sorrow is, yet it is more constant. Grief for sin is continual; whereas outward sorrow is but upon a sudden, though it seem to be more violent.

2. And again, *in regard of their valuing and prizing of earthly things,* there may be a sudden sorrow: for a child of God may, upon a sudden, overprize outward things, and esteem them at too high a rate; but yet after that, valuing things by good advice, they prize spiritual things far beyond outward; and therefore their sorrow and joy is more for spiritual things, because it is constant.

This I speak, not to cherish any neglect in any Christian, but for comfort to such as are troubled for it; therefore let such know, that God will not 'break the bruised reed, nor quench the smoking flax' (*Isa.* 42:3). If they have but a desire, and by conscientious use of means, do show their desire to be true, they shall have it at last, for Christ continues to make intercession for us; and if there were no weakness in us, what need Christ continue to make peace for us? for peace is made for those that fall out. Therefore, if there were no falling out between God and us, what need Christ to continue to make intercession for us? For these reasons, we see a child of God, for the present, may be more sensible of outward things than of spiritual.

Question. But here another question may be asked, How shall we know that we have sensibleness and pliableness, or not?

Answer. I answer, Easily, by applying of the soul unto objects, as 1., to God; 2., to his word; 3., to his works; 4., to man.

We may try our tenderness and pliableness of heart these four ways:

1. *To God.* As it is tender *from* God, so it is tender *for* God; for the three persons of the Trinity. He that has a tender heart cannot endure to dishonour God himself, or to hear others dishonour him, either by his own sins or by others' sins. He cannot endure to hear God's name blasphemed. So that they have a tender heart who, when they see Christ in his religion to be wronged, cannot choose but be affected with it.

So again, a man has a tender heart when he yields to the motions of the Holy Ghost. When the Spirit moves, and he yields, this shows there is a tender heart.

But a hard heart beats back all, and as a stone to the hammer, will not yield to any motion of God's Spirit.

2. Now, in the second place, to come downward, a tender heart is sensible in regard *of the word of God;* as, first, at the threatenings a true tender heart will tremble, 'To him will I look, even to him that is of a contrite and broken spirit, and trembleth at my words' (*Isa.* 66:2). A man that has a tender heart will tremble at the signs of the anger of God: 'Shall the lion roar, and the beasts of the forest not be afraid?' (*Amos* 3:4). Yes, they will stand still and tremble at the roaring of the lion; but much more will a tender heart tremble when God roars, and threatens vengeance. A tender heart will tremble when it hears of the terrors of the Lord at the day of judgment, as Paul did:

'Now knowing the terrors of the Lord, we persuade men' (*2 Cor.* 5:11). It forced him to be faithful in his office. This use the apostle Peter would have us make of it: 'That seeing all these things must be dissolved, what manner of persons ought we to be in holy conversation and godliness?' (*2 Pet.* 3:11). And so for the promises in the word. The heart is tender when the word of God rejoices a man above all things. How can the heart but melt at God's promises, for they are the sweetest things that can be. Therefore when a tender heart hears God's promises, it makes him to melt and be sensible of them.

Again, a tender heart will be pliable to any direction in the word. To God's call it will answer, 'Here I am; Lord, what will you have me to do?' As Isaiah, when he had once a tender heart, then 'Send me, Lord' (*Isa.* 6:8). So David to God's command, 'Seek my face,' answers, 'Your face, Lord, will I seek' (*Psa.* 27:8). There is a gracious echo of the soul to God in whatsoever he says in his word. And thus a true, tender heart yields to the word of God, and is fit to run on any errand.

3. Thirdly, By applying it *to the works of God;* for a tender heart quakes when it sees the judgment of God abroad upon others. It hastens to make its peace with God, and to meet him by repentance. So again, a tender heart rejoices at the mercy of God, for it sees something in it better than the thing itself; and that is the love of God, from which it proceeds.

4. Fourthly, A man may know his heart to be tender and sensible, in regard *of the*

estate of others, whether they be good or bad.
If they be wicked, he has a tender heart
for them; as David, 'Mine eyes gush out
with rivers of water, because men keep
not your law' (*Psa.* 119:136). So Paul says,
'There are many that walk inordinately,
of whom I have told you before, and now
tell you weeping' (*Phil.* 3:18). So Christ was
sensible of the misery of Jerusalem, wept
for it, and a little while after, shed his own
blood for it (*Matt.* 23:37). Thus had he a
tender heart. But when Christ looked to
God's decree, he says, 'Father, I thank you,
Lord of heaven and earth, that you have
hid these things from the wise and noble,
and have revealed them unto babes' (*Matt.*
11:25). And so likewise for those that are
good, in giving and forgiving; in giving,
they give not only the thing, but they give

their hearts and affections with it; and so in forgiving, they apprehend Christ's love in forgiving them; therefore they forgive others. So for works, will God have a tender heart to do anything, it will do it. If he will have it mourn, it will mourn; if to rejoice, it will rejoice; it is fit for every good work. By these marks we may know whether we have tender hearts or not.

But to *apply* this; How is this affection of Josiah in the hearts of men in these days? How many have melting hearts when they hear God blasphemed, and the religion of Christ wronged? How few are there that yield to the motions of the Spirit! We may take up a wonderful complaint of the hardness of men's hearts in these days, who never tremble at the word of God. Neither his promises, nor threatenings, nor commands will melt their hearts; but this is certain, that they which are not better under religion, by the means of grace, are much the worse. And how sensible are we of the church's miseries? For a tender heart is sensible of the miseries of the church, as being members of the same body, whereof Christ is the head. But men nowadays are so far from melting hearts, that they want[4] natural affection, as Paul foretells of such in the latter times (*1 Tim.* 4:1). They have less feelings of pity in them, when they hear how it goes with the church abroad, than very pagans and heathens. This shows they have no tender hearts, that they are not knit to Christ by faith, who is the head; nor to the church, the body, in love. How is your heart affected to men when they

---

[4] That is, 'want' in the sense of 'lack'.

commit any sin against God, as idolaters, swearers, drunkards, liars, and the like? Is it mercy to let these go on in their sins towards hell? No, this is cruelty; but mercy is to be showed unto them, in restraining men from their wicked courses. Therefore do not think you show mercy unto them by letting them alone in sin, but exhort and instruct them. Coldness and deadness is a spiritual disease in these days. But surely they that have the Spirit of God warming their hearts, are sensible of their own good and ill, and of the good and ill of the time.

Well, if you will know you have a tender heart, look to God, look to his word, to his works, to yourselves, and others; and so you shall know whether you have tender hearts or not.

Question. But here may be another question asked, How shall men recover themselves, when they are subject to this hardness, deadness, and insensibleness? If after examination a man find himself to be thus, how shall he recover himself out of this estate? I answer:

Answer. 1. First, As when things are cold we bring them to the fire to heat and melt, so *we bring our cold hearts to the fire of the love of Christ;* we consider of our sins against Christ, and of Christ's love towards us; dwell upon this meditation. Think what great love Christ has showed unto us, and how little we have deserved, and this will make our hearts to melt and be as pliable as wax before the sun.

2. Secondly, If you will have this tender and melting heart, then *use the means of grace;* be always under the sunshine of the gospel. Be under God's sunshine, that he may melt your heart; be constant in good means; and

help one another. 'We must provoke one another daily, lest any be hardened through the deceitfulness of sin' (*Heb.* 3:13). Physicians love not to give physic to themselves. So a man is not always fit to help himself when he is not right; but good company is fit to do it. 'Did not our hearts burn within us while he talked with us?' said the two disciples, holding communion each with other at Emmaus (*Luke* 24:32). For then Christ comes and makes a third, joins with them, and so makes their hearts burn within them. So Christ says, 'Where two or three are met together in his name, he is in the midst of them' (*Matt.* 18:20). Now they were under the promise, therefore he affords his presence. Where two hold communion together, there Christ will make a third. Therefore let us use the help of others, seeing David could not recover himself, being a prophet, but he must have a Nathan to help him (*2 Sam.* 12:7). Therefore if we would recover ourselves from hard and insensible hearts, let us use the help one of another.

3. Thirdly, *We must with boldness and reverence challenge the covenant of grace;* for this is the covenant that God has made with us, to give us tender hearts, hearts of flesh, as Ezekiel 11:19, 'I will give them one heart, and put a new spirit within them; I will take away the stony hearts out of their bodies, and I will give them a heart of flesh.' Now seeing this is a covenant God has made, to give us fleshly hearts and to take away our stony, let us challenge him with his promise, and go to him by prayer. Entreat him to give you a fleshly heart; go to him, wait his time, for that is the best

time. Therefore wait though he do not hear at first. These are the means to bring tenderness of heart.

Now, that you may be stirred up to this duty, namely, to get a soft and tender heart, mark here:

1. First, *What an excellent thing a tender heart is.* God has promised to dwell in such an heart, and it is an excellent thing to have God dwell in our hearts, as he has promised, 'For thus says he that is high and excellent, he that inhabits eternity, whose name is the Holy One: I will dwell in the high and holy place, and with him also that is of a contrite and humble spirit, to revive the spirit of the humble, and to give life to them that are of a contrite heart' (*Isa.* 57:15). So Isaiah 66:2: 'To him will I look, even to him that is poor and contrite in spirit, and trembles at my words.' Now God having

promised to dwell where there is a soft heart, and no hardness, no rocks to keep him out; can God come into a heart without a blessing? Can he be separated from goodness, who is goodness itself? When the heart therefore is pliable and thus tender, there is an immediate communion between the soul and God; and can that heart be miserable that has communion with God? Surely not.

2. Secondly, Consider *that this fits a man for the end for which he was created*. A man is never fit for that end for which he was made, but when he has a tender heart; and what are we redeemed for, but that we should serve God? And who is fit to be put in the service of God but he that has begged a tender heart of God?

3. Thirdly, To stir you up to labour for this, consider *that a tender heart is fit for any*

blessedness. It is capable of any beatitude. What makes a man blessed in anything but a tender heart? This will make a man to hear the word, to read, to show mercies to others. 'Blessed are the poor in spirit', says Christ, 'for theirs is the kingdom of heaven.' A tender heart is blessed, because that only hears God's word, and does it; and it is always a merciful heart, and therefore blessed.

4. Again, Consider *the wretched estate of a heart contrary, that is not tender, and will not yield*. Oh what a wonderful hardness would the heart of man grow to, if we do not follow it with means to soften it! What a fearful thing was it to see what strange things fell out at Christ's death, what darkness there was, what thunders and lightnings. The veil of the temple rent, the

sun was turned into darkness, the graves opened, and the dead did rise, yet notwithstanding none of these would make the hypocritical Pharisees to tremble, but they mocked at it, although it made a very heathen man confess it the work of God (*Matt.* 27:45-54). For a ceremonial hypocrite is more hard than a Turk, Jew, or Pagan. All the judgments of God upon Pharaoh were not so great as hardness of heart. The papists, after they have been at their superstitious devotion, are fittest for powder plots and treasons,[5] because their hearts are so much more hardened. What fearful things may a man come to, if he give way

[5] An allusion to the The Gunpowder Plot of 1605, in earlier centuries often called the Gunpowder Treason Plot, which was a failed assassination attempt against King James I of England (James VI of Scotland) by a group of provincial English Roman Catholics which included the infamous Guy Fawkes.

to hardness of heart! He may come to an estate like the devil, yea, worse than Judas, for he had some sensibleness of his sin; he confessed he had sinned in betraying the innocent blood. But many of these hypocrites have no sensibleness at all, which is a fearful thing. Eli's children hearkened not to the voice of their father, because that the Lord had a purpose to destroy them (*1 Sam.* 2:25). So it is in this case a shrewd sign that God will destroy those that are so insensible that nothing will work upon them. But these hypocrites shall be sensible one day, when they shall wish they were as insensible as in their lifetime they were. But it will be an unfruitful repentance to repent in hell; for there a man shall get no benefit by his repentance, seeing *there* they cannot shake off the execution of God's judgment, as they shake off the threatenings of his judgments *here*. Well, to this fearful end, before it be long, must everyone that has a hard heart come, unless they repent. Therefore let everyone be persuaded to labour for a tender, pliable, yielding, and sensible heart here, else we shall have it hereafter against our wills, when it will do us no good; for then hypocrites shall be sensible against their wills, though they would not be sensible in this life.

And thus I have done with the first inward cause in Josiah that moved God so to respect him, namely, *tenderness of heart*.

OTHER
POCKET PURITANS

OTHER BOOKS BY
RICHARD SIBBES

The Bruised Reed, 138pp., paperback
ISBN: 978 0 85151 740 7

The Works of Richard Sibbes
ISBN (7-volume set): 978 085151 398 0

Sibbes excelled as a comforter of the troubled and doubting, but he also possessed the rare gift of illuminating every passage of Scripture he handled by drawing out its significance for his hearers and readers. All who have an appetite for helpful and faithful biblical preaching will treasure these volumes.

Support the work of the Trust and keep abreast of all our latest publications too by subscribing to *The Banner of Truth* magazine. Available in paper and electronic formats, it is full of interesting articles, book reviews, news and comment. For more details about how to receive the magazine please visit our website:

www.banneroftruth.co.uk

For more details of all Banner publications,
including the Puritan Paperback series and
our reprints of the works of the Puritans,
please visit our website:

www.banneroftruth.co.uk

THE BANNER OF TRUTH TRUST

3 Murrayfield Road,
Edinburgh EH12 6EL
UK

P O Box 621, Carlisle,
PA 17013,
USA

www.banneroftruth.co.uk